APRIL 2016

Iran in a Reconnecting Eurasia

Foreign Economic and Security Interests

AUTHOR
Mohsen Milani

EDITOR
Jeffrey Mankoff

Eurasia from the Outside In

A REPORT OF THE
CSIS RUSSIA AND EURASIA PROGRAM

CSIS | CENTER FOR STRATEGIC &
INTERNATIONAL STUDIES

ROWMAN &
LITTLEFIELD

Lanham • Boulder • New York • London

About CSIS

For over 50 years, the Center for Strategic and International Studies (CSIS) has worked to develop solutions to the world's greatest policy challenges. Today, CSIS scholars are providing strategic insights and bipartisan policy solutions to help decisionmakers chart a course toward a better world.

CSIS is a nonprofit organization headquartered in Washington, D.C. The Center's 220 full-time staff and large network of affiliated scholars conduct research and analysis and develop policy initiatives that look into the future and anticipate change.

Founded at the height of the Cold War by David M. Abshire and Admiral Arleigh Burke, CSIS was dedicated to finding ways to sustain American prominence and prosperity as a force for good in the world. Since 1962, CSIS has become one of the world's preeminent international institutions focused on defense and security; regional stability; and transnational challenges ranging from energy and climate to global health and economic integration.

Thomas J. Pritzker was named chairman of the CSIS Board of Trustees in November 2015. Former U.S. deputy secretary of defense John J. Hamre has served as the Center's president and chief executive officer since 2000.

CSIS does not take specific policy positions; accordingly, all views expressed herein should be understood to be solely those of the author(s).

ISBN: 978-1-4422-5936-2 (pb); 978-1-4422-5937-9 (eBook)

Center for Strategic & International Studies
1616 Rhode Island Avenue, NW
Washington, DC 20036
202-887-0200 | www.**csis**.org

Rowman & Littlefield
4501 Forbes Boulevard
Lanham, MD 20706
301-459-3366 | www.**rowman**.com

Contents

iv   Preface

vi   Acknowledgments

1   CHAPTER 1 | The View from Tehran

6   CHAPTER 2 | Iran's Foreign Economic and Security Policy

22   CHAPTER 3 | Iran in a Reconnecting Eurasia

25   CHAPTER 4 | Conclusion

28   About the Author

Preface

In January 2014, the CSIS Russia and Eurasia Program launched its Eurasia Initiative. The vast Eurasian landmass, stretching from China in the east to Europe in the west and from the Arctic Ocean in the north to the Indian Ocean in the south, includes some of the world's most powerful and dynamic states, as well as some of the world's most intractable challenges. Scholars and analysts are accustomed to focusing separately on Eurasia's various regions—Europe, the former Soviet Union, East Asia, South Asia, and Southeast Asia—rather than on the interactions between them. The goal of this initiative is to focus on these interactions, while analyzing and understanding Eurasia in a comprehensive way.

Today, more than any time since the collapse of the Silk Road five centuries ago, understanding these individual regions is impossible without also understanding the connections between them. Over the past two decades, Eurasia has begun to slowly reconnect, with the emergence of new trade relationships and transit infrastructures, as well as the integration of Russia, China, and India into the global economy. Even as this reconnection is under way, the center of economic dynamism in Eurasia, and in the world as a whole, continues shifting to the East. The impact of these shifts is potentially enormous, but they remain poorly understood because of intellectual and bureaucratic stovepiping in government and the broader analytic community.

Following its twin report series on Central Asia and on the South Caucasus, respectively, the CSIS Russia and Eurasia Program is now releasing papers in a third series we are informally calling "Eurasia from the Outside In." If the first two Eurasia Initiative report series focused on how economic connectivity and shifting political alignments looked from the interior of Eurasia, the current series focuses on the perspectives of the large, powerful countries that make up the periphery of the Eurasian landmass, namely China, India, Iran, Russia, and Turkey, as well as the European Union. The six reports in this series, each written by a leading local scholar of Eurasia, seek to provide insight into where Eurasia fits among the foreign economic and security priorities of these major powers.

While the most visible components of Eurasia's reconnection are infrastructure projects, the longer term result has been a reshuffling of relations between the post-Soviet states of Central

Asia and the South Caucasus on the one hand, and the major regional powers on the other. When the states of Central Asia and the South Caucasus became independent 25 years ago, they were closely tied to Russia. Over the past two and a half decades, they have developed a complex web of linkages to the other Eurasian powers, who themselves have devoted increased resources and attention to Eurasia in the years since the Soviet collapse. Russia still remains the dominant security provider in Central Asia and most of the South Caucasus. However China, the European Union, India, Iran, and Turkey all play major, if still evolving, roles in the region as well.

The scholars we have commissioned to write these reports bring a deep knowledge of their respective countries as well as a strong understanding of developments across Eurasia. While they are addressing a common set of questions, their answers and perspectives often diverge. Our goal is not consensus. Rather, it is to provide the best possible analysis of the roles these states are playing in shaping Eurasia's reconnection. We chose to seek out scholars from the countries being studied so that these reports would not be U.S.-centric, but would rather throw light on how Ankara, Beijing, Brussels, Moscow, New Delhi, and Tehran conceive of their respective interests and strategies in Eurasia.

With this report series, and indeed with the Eurasia Initiative more generally, we hope to encourage analysts and policymakers to think about Eurasia in a holistic way. Eurasia is much more than just the periphery of the old Soviet Union: it is a patchwork of states and peoples whose relationships are shifting rapidly. It is Central Asia, but it is also Europe; the South Caucasus but also India. Most importantly, it is the connections that are emerging and developing between these various states and regions. Our "Eurasia from the Inside Out" report series highlights the extent to which the comparatively small states at Eurasia's center have become a focal point for the economic and political engagement of the much larger powers surrounding them, and hence why these states continue to matter for global peace and prosperity.

Acknowledgments

I am most grateful to my wife, Ramak Milani, without whose love, support, and encouragement I would not have been able to write this report. She conducted some research and read the entire paper, enriching it with her astute commentaries. I am thankful to Parandoosh Sadeghinia, our talented graduate assistant at the University of South Florida (USF) World's Center for Strategic and Diplomatic Studies, for her research on this project. It has been a great pleasure to work with the wonderful and professional staff of the Russia and Eurasia Program of the Center for Strategic and International Studies. Dr. Jeffrey Mankoff read the paper and greatly improved its quality by asking probing questions and polishing it. It was Dr. Andrew Kuchins who made this project possible.

This report is made possible by the generous support of the Smith Richardson Foundation, the Carnegie Corporation of New York, the Ministry of Foreign Affairs of the Republic of Kazakhstan, and Carlos Bulgheroni. We are also extremely grateful for program support provided by the Carnegie Corporation of New York to the CSIS Russia and Eurasia Program.

The View from Tehran

The disintegration of the Soviet Union gave Iran an historic opportunity to emerge as a regional power in Central Asia (Kazakhstan, Kyrgyzstan, Tajikistan, Turkmenistan, and Uzbekistan) and the South Caucasus (Azerbaijan, Armenia, and Georgia). After all, a portion of those two regions was an integral part of Iran until the early eighteenth century, when Iran was forced to cede it to Russia.[1] Iran also has deep-rooted historical, cultural, linguistic, and religious ties with many of the new republics that emerged from the ruins of the Soviet Union. The discovery of enormous reserves of natural gas and oil in the 1980s in and around the Caspian Sea, located on Iran's northern borders, provided additional, and irresistible, incentives for Iran to expand its influence throughout the region.

Iran has the ambition as well as the resources to become a major regional power and a hub for distribution of Caspian hydrocarbons to international markets. Iran has the world's second and fourth largest reserves of natural gas and oil, respectively. Its gross domestic product (GDP) and population are only slightly less than those of the eight countries of the South Caucasus and Central Asia combined (Table 1.1).[2] Strategically, too, Iran is ideally located to provide the shortest possible route for connecting the energy-rich Caspian Sea and landlocked Central Asia to the warm waters of the Persian Gulf and ultimately to international markets.

---

1. As a result of losing two wars to Russia, the disastrous Golestan Treaty of 1813 and the Turkmenchay Treaty of 1828 were imposed on Iran. Consequently, Iran ceded to Russia what is roughly equivalent to the Republic of Armenia, most of the Republic of Azerbaijan, eastern Georgia, Dagestan, Nakhchivan Autonomous Republic, and a few other places. For details, see Firuz Kazemzadeh, *Russia and Britain in Persia: Imperial Ambitions in Qajar Iran* (London: I. B. Taurus, 2013).

2. Iran's main competitors in the two regions are China, Russia, and Turkey. In terms of world ranking for the GDP (billions of dollars) in 2014, China was ranked second ($10,360), Russia eighth ($1,860), Turkey eighteenth ($799), and Iran twenty-ninth ($415), respectively. See "World Databank: Gross Domestic Product 2014," World Bank, http://databank .worldbank.org/data/download/GDP.xls. In terms of the size of the population in 2014, China was ranked number one (1.36 billion), Russia ninth (143.8 million), Iran seventeenth (78.1 million), and Turkey eighteenth (75.9 million), respectively. See "Databank: Population 2014," World Bank, December 22, 2015, http://databank.worldbank.org/data/download /POP.pdf.

Despite these advantages, Iran has not emerged as a regional power in Eurasia as it has in the Persian Gulf and the Levant. Nor has Iran become a major hydrocarbon hub for its Eurasian neighbors, though it does remain an influential player whose role in the region cannot be ignored.

Iran faces some formidable obstacles in both the South Caucasus and Central Asia. Tehran has no enemies in the region, but nor does it have any dependable strategic allies. If anything, Iran continues to suffer from a debilitating strategic isolation. Unable to articulate realistic strategic goals, Tehran has often acted tactically and reactively. Most important, in the fateful game of building pipelines to connect the Caspian Sea to global markets, Iran has been marginalized, if not altogether excluded. Still Iran has engaged in an assortment of joint small and medium-size investment projects with some of the Caspian states, including small pipelines for oil and gas transport and power-generating facilities, as well as railways, roads, and tunnels. But Iran's trade with and investments in Eurasia remain small as a percentage of its total exports and foreign investment.

Iran faces other obstacles as well. China and particularly Russia have vital national interests in the South Caucasus and Central Asia that have not always been compatible with Iran's. Beijing and Moscow have at best reluctantly tolerated a limited expansion of Iranian influence, while Russia in particular is vigilant about protecting its immense energy exports to Europe from Iranian competition. Tehran, ever more anxious to use these two powers to counterbalance the United States, has never sought to challenge them directly. Moreover, both Beijing and Moscow have time and again demonstrated that they would support Tehran only if it does not endanger their own relations with Washington. They have effectively used Iran as a powerful bargaining chip in their negotiations with the United States. In addition, Turkey has fiercely competed with Iran for regional influence. In fact, Turkey, a member of the North Atlantic Treaty Organization (NATO), has benefited enormously from Western sanctions imposed on Iran. Nor have the states of the South Caucasus and Central Asia themselves been enthusiastic about developing close strategic ties with Iran, fearing that friendship with Tehran would undermine their own developing relations with the United States and anger Moscow and Beijing as well.

Ultimately, however, what has most prevented Iran from playing a major role in the South Caucasus and Central Asia has been the effective U.S. strategy of containment and the suffocating sanctions it imposed over Iran's nuclear program. Iran's own anti-Americanism has also damaged its interests in the region. For the past two decades, Tehran has spent substantial resources in the Levant and the Persian Gulf regions in a quixotic effort to roll back American influence. The preoccupation with those two regions, coupled with Washington's sanctions policy, sapped a disproportionate amount of Iran's resources, leading Tehran to neglect its interests in Eurasia.

However, the landmark nuclear deal between Iran and six global powers provides a unique opportunity for Iran to make some necessary changes in the direction of its foreign policy and reformulate its policies toward Central Asia and South Caucasus, potentially becoming a regional power.

BURDEN OF THE ISLAMIC REVOLUTION ON IRANIAN REGIONAL POLICIES

Iran developed its policies toward the South Caucasus and Central Asia in the face of numerous constraints.

The Islamic Republic, which regards the United States an existential threat, has indefatigably struggled to deter the United States by exporting its revolution, undermining U.S. allies, developing asymmetric warfare strategies and retaliatory capabilities, and creating proxies and spheres of influence beyond its borders, in such places as Lebanon and Syria.[3]

The founder of the Islamic Republic, Ayatollah Ruhollah Khomeini, was reluctant to antagonize Moscow and hoped to use the USSR as a balance against the United States, despite the Soviet Union's official embrace of atheism. During the Soviet era, Iran had no direct contact with the republics of the South Caucasus and Central Asia and dealt exclusively with Moscow. While Ayatollah Khomeini talked of exporting Iran's Islamic Revolution, he did not seek to incite the large Muslim populations of the Soviet Union against the Kremlin. And when the Soviet Union invaded Afghanistan in 1979, he rhetorically condemned the occupation and demanded a Soviet withdrawal, but he adamantly refused to join the Islamabad-Riyadh-Washington axis to arm the Afghan mujahideen fighting the Soviets.[4]

Ayatollah Khomeini died in 1988, a year after the war with Iraq ended. A few years later, the United States sent troops to the Persian Gulf to end Iraq's occupation of Kuwait, and the Soviet Union disintegrated. These two momentous events created a security nightmare for Tehran on its southern border, as the United States was now able to station thousands of troops around the Persian Gulf. Of course, the Soviet collapse also created new opportunities for Iran to project power on its northern borders, where several new republics with historic ties to Iran had just achieved their independence.[5] Iran, therefore, had to formulate new strategies toward these newly independent republics and at the same time recalibrate its foreign policy to a new unipolar world order with the United States at its apex.

Shortly after the Soviet collapse, then Iranian president Ali Akbar Hashemi Rafsanjani prudently sought to reduce tensions with the United States by restarting economic cooperation. He sent conciliatory messages to Washington and stayed neutral in the First Persian Gulf War, when the United States forcibly expelled Iraqi forces from Kuwait. He also agreed to a $1 billion oil deal with Conoco, the largest deal with a U.S. energy firm since the Islamic Revolution. Although President Bill Clinton supported the deal at first, he ultimately succumbed to congressional pressure and vetoed it. He also signed an executive order banning U.S. companies from investing in the Iranian oil and gas sectors, as well as the Iran-Libya Sanctions Act (ILSA) that threatened

---

3. Mohsen Milani, "Tehran's Take: Understanding Iran's U.S. Policy," *Foreign Affairs* (July/August 2009), 46–62.

4. Mohsen Milani, "Iran's Policy Towards Afghanistan," *Middle East Journal* 60, no. 2 (Spring 2006): 235–256.

5. Shireen T. Hunter, *Iran's Foreign Policy in the Post-Soviet Era: Resisting the New International Order* (Santa Barbara, CA: Praeger Publishers, 2010).

Table 1.1 Total Population, Total GDP, Total Crude Oil Reserves, and Total Natural Gas Reserves for the Countries in Central Asia and the South Caucasus and for Iran

	Armenia	Azerbaijan	Georgia	Kazakhstan	Kyrgyzstan	Tajikistan	Turkmenistan	Uzbekistan	Total for CASA	Iran
Population (In Thousands) 2015	3,018	9,754	4,000	17,625	5,940	8,482	5,374	29,893	84,086	79,109
Total GDP (Millions of Dollars, 2014)	10,882	75,198	16,530	212,248	7,404	9,242	47,932	62,644	442,080	415,339
Crude Oil Reserves (Billions of Barrels, 2015)	0	7	0	30	0.040	0.012	0.600	0.594	38.246	157.800
Proved Reserves of Natural Gas (Trillion Cubic Feet, 2015)	0	35	0	85	0.200	0.200	265	65	450.400	1,201.382

Sources: For population, see United Nations, *World Population Prospects: The 2015 Revision* (New York: United Nations, 2015), http://esa.un.org /unpd/wpp/publications/files/key_findings_wpp_2015.pdf; for oil, see U.S. Energy Information Administration (EIA), *International Energy Statistics 2011–2015: Petroleum* (Washington, DC: EIA, 2015), http://www.eia.gov/cfapps/ipdbproject/IEDIndex3.cfm?tid=5&pid=57&aid=6; for natural gas, see U.S. EIA, *International Energy Statistics 2011–2015: Natural Gas* (Washington, DC: EIA, 2015), http://www.eia.gov/cfapps/ipdbproject/IEDIndex3 .cfm?tid=3&pid=3&aid=6; for GDP, see "Databank: Gross domestic product 2014," World Bank, http://databank.worldbank.org/data/download/GDP.xls.

sanctions on any foreign company investing more than $20 million in the Iranian energy sector.[6]

These actions by Washington created insurmountable obstacles to Iran's efforts to boost its influence in the newly independent states of Eurasia. Although Rafsanjani quickly recognized the independence of the new republics and developed good neighborly relations with them, Iran was sidelined as new oil and gas reserves were discovered in the Caspian Sea and huge pipeline projects were designed, mostly by powerful Western oil companies.

The terrorist attacks on the U.S. homeland by al Qaeda on September 11, 2001 created a fleeting hope for Iran-U.S. rapprochement, as both worked together to dismantle the Taliban regime in Afghanistan. But President George W. Bush's inclusion of Iran as a member of the "Axis of Evil" in his January 2002 State of the Union speech intensified the cold war between Washington and Tehran. The animosity between the two reached its height during the presidency of Mahmoud Ahmadinejad (2005–2013) in Iran. As Ahmadinejad accelerated Iran's nuclear program and pursued a confrontational (and ultimately unproductive) foreign policy, the West imposed ever more crippling sanctions on Iran and restrained even further Iran's ability to expand its influence into Eurasia.

In 2012, Robert Blake, then the U.S. assistant secretary of state for South and Central Asian affairs, succinctly captured the consequences of Iran's commitment to an anti-American foreign policy on its ability to project power in Eurasia: "Let me just say that consistent with America's sanctions on Iran, the United States is encouraging all of the countries of the region to avoid trade and other transactions with the government of Iran in order to pressure Iran to engage with the international community about its concerns about Iran's nuclear program."[7] In reality, Washington had consistently, and to some degree successfully, contained Iran in Eurasia since the Soviet collapse.

There were, however, other reasons for Iran's inability to project power in Eurasia. The states of the South Caucasus and Central Asia themselves were hardly enthusiastic about developing close ties with Tehran, as they were eager to gravitate toward the West, an ambition that closer ties with Tehran would have jeopardized. Moreover, some countries, such as Azerbaijan and Tajikistan, were genuinely nervous about the export of Iran's Islamic Revolution. Nevertheless, all countries in the two regions have maintained diplomatic relations with Tehran, though at a level designed not to antagonize Moscow, Beijing, or Ankara.

---

6. Kenneth M. Pollack, *The Persian Puzzle: Deciphering the Twenty-five-Year Conflict Between the United States and Iran* (New York: Random House, 2004).

7. As quoted in Monica Witt, "Why Tajikistan Won't Abandon the Islamic Republic of Iran," *International Affairs Review* (April 2, 2012), http://www.iar-gwu.org/node/398. Although the comment was made in 2012, this has been the U.S. policy since 1991.

02

Iran's Foreign Economic and Security Policy

As significant as Central Asia and the South Caucasus are, relations with these regions have never been among the top priorities of Iran's foreign policy. Beyond its global standoff with the United States, relations with the countries of the Persian Gulf and the Levant and with Turkey remain the top regional priorities for Iran.

Based on declarations by Iranian officials and published documents,[1] Iran seems to have pursued seven broad regional goals toward the South Caucasus and Central Asia in the past quarter century.

1. To develop political, economic, and cultural relations with all the states of the South Caucasus and Central Asia while becoming a major regional power in the two areas;

2. To finalize a favorable resolution regarding the legal status of the Caspian Sea in order to protect and exploit reserves of natural gas, oil, and other resources;

3. To undermine the Western sanctions regime and neutralize the U.S. containment strategy by strengthening ties and initiating joint projects with the states of Central Asia and the South Caucasus, including through participation in regional organizations such as the Shanghai Cooperation Organization (SCO) and the Economic Cooperation Organization (ECO), and engaging in a variety of swap and bartering deals with the regional states;

4. To prevent any grave security threat to Iran emanating from any of the South Caucasus or Central Asian states and block the United States from establishing military bases in the two regions;

---

1. Abbas Maleki, one of Iran's best experts on Central Asia and the South Caucuses, discusses Iranian policy toward Central Asia. See Abbas Maleki, "Iran, Central Asia, and Afghanistan: Recent Developments" (presentation, Central Asia Caucasus Institute, School for Advanced International Studies, Johns Hopkins University, Baltimore, MD, April 5, 2006), http://belfercenter.ksg.harvard.edu/files/iranandcentralasia.pdf. See also Abbas Maleki, "Iran and Turan: Apropos of Iran's Relations with Central Asia and the Caucasian Republics," *Central Asia and the Caucasus* 5 (2001), http://www.ca-c.org/journal/eng-05-2001/11.malprimen.shtml.

5. To become a major energy hub for the two regions, exporting its natural gas and oil to Europe, and connecting, through pipelines, landlocked Central Asia and the Caspian Sea to the Persian Gulf and the Gulf of Oman;

6. To expand and connect its railway networks, roads, and tunnels to revive the old Silk Road, connecting Iran to China and India through Central Asia and to Europe through the South Caucasus;

7. To cooperate and collaborate with the states of the South Caucasus and Central Asia to combat violent jihadism and terrorism.

Like other states, Iran has used all the instruments of power at its disposal to expand its influence and project power in Central Asia and the South Caucasus. But Tehran has used much less of its limited military power in this region than it has in the Persian Gulf and the Levant. Instead, it has taken advantage of its favorable geostrategic location to provide transit routes to the landlocked countries in Central Asia to reach international waters and engaged with the regional states in joint economic and developmental projects. And Iran has used its soft power, mainly through cultural exchanges and Persian radio and television programs, to present its perspectives, explain its policies, and expand its influence.

In contrast to its behavior in the Persian Gulf and the Levant, Iran has behaved much more like a classic Westphalian state than a revolutionary state in its dealing with the South Caucasus and Central Asia. Iran's policies in the region have been more pragmatic, more business-oriented, and considerably less ideological than its policies toward immediate neighbors in other regions such as Iraq and Saudi Arabia. National interests, more palpably than spreading or exporting revolutionary Islam or Shi'aism, have shaped and defined Iranian policies in Eurasia.

There are five compelling reasons for this discernible pragmatism in Iranian policies toward the two regions.

First, unlike the situation in the Middle East, there has been no serious security threat to Iran originating from Eurasia, even though relations with the eight states of the South Caucasus and Central Asia have not been free of tension. Iran continues, for instance, to have serious disagreements about the legal status of the Caspian Sea with the other littoral states and remains highly critical of Azerbaijan for its friendly relations with Israel and invocation of irredentist claims against Iran itself. But these controversies have never reached the level of the threat posed, for example, by Iraq under Saddam Hussein or Afghanistan under Taliban rule.

Second, all the Central Asian countries have predominantly Sunni populations and secular governments. In the first decade after the Islamic Revolution, Iran tried to export its revolution, particularly to states with a substantial Shi'a population, including several of the Persian Gulf countries and Lebanon. Moreover, fighting Israel has been a key priority of Iranian foreign policy. It is not accidental that the most elite unit of the Islamic Revolutionary Guards Corps (IRGC), which is chiefly responsible for spreading the Islamic Revolution, is named the Qods, or Jerusalem. Simply put, Iran has hardly been interested, or had the resources, to export its revolution to the unfavorable ground of Central Asia.

The South Caucasus in this regard is more complex. Armenia, which has excellent relations with Iran, is a Christian country and totally immunized against the ideals of the Islamic Revolution. Georgia, another Christian country, has never feared the spread of Iran's revolutionary message and has developed friendly relations with Iran. Iran has had a contentious relationship, however, with predominantly Shi'a (though secular) Azerbaijan. Iran made some feeble attempts to push its revolutionary agenda in Azerbaijan, and Baku reciprocated by calling for unification with the Iranian province of Azerbaijan. Much to their mutual credit, both countries have prudently managed their discord and have even become reluctant partners in a few energy projects.

Third, with the rise of violent Sunni extremism and violent jihadism, including the brief ascendancy of the Taliban in Afghanistan, Iran has been much more focused and interested in combating Sunni extremism in Central Asia and the South Caucasus than exporting its own brand of revolutionary Shi'ism.

Fourth, Iran has been exceptionally wary of disturbing the status quo within the states of the South Caucasus and Central Asia. For one thing, Iran does not wish to antagonize China and Russia, both of which do have vital interests in the region. Iran has relied on both Moscow and Beijing to balance against the United States and has little interest in alienating them. Moreover, both Russia and Iran would prefer the status quo in Eurasia over turmoil and chaos, which would easily pave the way for Western military intervention, which both adamantly oppose.

Fifth and finally, Iran's participation in the Economic Cooperation Organization and the Shanghai Cooperation Organization has somewhat moderated its regional policies. Although Iran is active in the Non-Aligned Movement and in the Organization of Islamic Cooperation, the only regional organizations in which Tehran actively participates are the ECO and SCO (Tehran is eager to become a full member of the SCO). Tehran is reluctant to jeopardize its standing in these two regional organizations, which confer on it a measure of international legitimacy, by disrupting the status quo in their member states.[2]

Iran's determination to minimize tension and deescalate any emerging conflict with Central Asia and the South Caucasus countries has generally been effective. Today, Tehran has cordial and friendly relations with all the countries in these two regions. In fact, Iran's northern borders have remained relatively safe. The two exceptions are the lingering dispute over the legal status of the Caspian Sea (known in Iran as the Khazar Sea) between Iran and the other four littoral states,[3] and Iran's political conflict with Azerbaijan.

---

2. Iran is an active member of the ECO, an intergovernmental regional organization founded by Iran, Turkey, and Pakistan in 1985 to promote economic cooperation. The ECO's official membership has expanded to include Azerbaijan and the five Central Asian countries. Iran also has been lobbying very hard to change its current status from "observer" to "full member" in the SCO, whose members include China, Russia, Kazakhstan, Kyrgyzstan, Uzbekistan, and Tajikistan. China and to a lesser extent Russia had opposed Iranian full membership in order not to antagonize the West. With the historic nuclear agreement, it is likely that Iran will become a full member.

3. The other littoral states are Azerbaijan, Kazakhstan, Turkmenistan, and Russia.

CASPIAN SEA

Persia was the dominant power in the Caspian Sea region until the 1720 Treaty of Rasht between the Persian and Russian empires. The treaty provided for freedom of commerce and navigation for both sides. Although Nader Shah Afshar (1736–1747) built a relatively powerful naval force in that sea in the futile hope of regaining lost Persian influence, the decline of Iranian power accelerated after his premature death.[4] The next decisive event was the Peace and Friendship Treaty signed in 1921 between the Bolshevik regime in Moscow and Iran. That treaty provided the legal framework governing the Caspian Sea until the collapse of the Soviet Union in 1991. The treaty gave both countries equal navigational and fishing rights and forbade the presence of foreign powers in the sea. The treaty, however, was rather ambiguous in respect to the way the natural resources of the sea were to be shared or divided between the two countries.[5]

After the fall of the Soviet Union, Iran found itself having to share the Caspian Sea with Russia and the three newly formed littoral states of Azerbaijan, Kazakhstan, and Turkmenistan. Initially, Tehran hoped to maintain the 1921 treaty giving Iran jurisdiction over one-half of the sea, while the other half would be divided among the other four littoral states. Discoveries of new oil and gas reserves in the Caspian turned the controversy over the legal status of that sea into a major dispute, with huge financial ramifications for all the littoral states as well as for Western oil companies. Negotiations have yet to produce a legal agreement, which has been most disadvantageous to Iran.

Anxious to sustain its close relationship with Russia in the years since 1991, Iran has significantly softened, if not surrendered, its original position in the subsequent negotiations.[6] Moscow and Tehran are in agreement about preventing ships from nonlittoral states from accessing the Caspian Sea. Their positions regarding sharing the resources of the Caspian, however, diverge radically. In a 2002 meeting in Moscow, Russia proposed that Iran should possess only 13 percent of the riches of the Caspian Sea, based on its share of the entire coastline. Iran rejected this proposal and instead advocated an equal division of the sea among the five littoral states, or 20 percent for each one of the five littoral states.[7] The marathon negotiations have yet to produce a final agreement.

---

4. Nader Shah Afshar was the last Persian conqueror who rose to power in a chaotic period in Iranian history. He unified the country, reinstituted the Persian Empire, and expanded Iranian power to Armenia, Azerbaijan, Georgia, Turkmenistan, Tajikistan, and Uzbekistan. See Laurence Lockhart, *Nadir Shah: A Critical Study Based Mainly Upon Contemporary Sources* (London: Luzac, 1938).

5. Barbara Janusz, "The Caspian Sea: Legal Status and Regime Problems," Chatham House, August 2005, 2, https://www.chathamhouse.org/sites/files/chathamhouse/public/Research/Russia%20and%20Eurasia/bp0805caspian.pdf.

6. For a comprehensive discussion of the legal status of the Caspian Sea, see Guive Mirfendereski, *A Diplomatic History of the Caspian Sea* (New York: Palgrave, 2001). Guive argues that Iran has surrendered its rights. See chapters 39–42.

7. See Mansour Kashfi, "Iran yields to Russia in talks over Caspian resources," *Oil and Gas Journal* (February 2, 2015), http://www.ogj.com/articles/print/volume-113/issue-2/general-interest/iran-yields-to-russia-in-talks-over-caspian-resources.html.

AZERBAIJAN

In the absence of a final legal agreement on the status of the Caspian, Russia, Kazakhstan, and Azerbaijan have agreed to use median lines to demarcate their respective littoral borders, an approach Iran has rejected. While this disagreement has had no practical ramifications for Iran's relations with Russia and Kazakhstan, it has generated discord with Azerbaijan regarding sovereignty over the rich Araz-Alov-Sharg oil and gas field, known in Iran as Alborz. The field, managed by BP and located 90 miles southeast of Baku, is the second largest in Azerbaijan with gas reserves estimated at 700 billion cubic meters (bcm) of gas, plus 90 million cubic meters of gas condensate, and capable of producing up to 8 bcm of gas per year.[8] The dispute reached a critical juncture when an Iranian naval ship reportedly threatened a BP exploration ship, which Azerbaijan claimed was operating in its territorial waters.[9] The incident, which was resolved peacefully, had symbolic importance as Azerbaijan, supported by the United States and the West, has continued to exploit the field in the absence of an agreement on demarcation.

Baku's pro-Western policies have paid huge dividends over the past two decades, but have also been a source of tension with Tehran. The 1,099-mile-long Baku-Tbilisi-Ceyhan (BTC) oil pipeline, operated by a multinational consortium that includes several major Western oil companies,[10] transports up to a million barrel of oil daily from the Azeri-Chirag-Guneshli field in the Caspian Sea through Georgia and Turkey to Turkey's Mediterranean coast.[11] It is not clear if Iran's exclusion from the pivotal pipeline was related to Iran's anti-American policies or was based on technical practicality.

Resource disputes between Iran and Azerbaijan have also erupted over the contested Shah Deniz natural gas field in the Caspian Sea. The South Caucasus gas pipeline, which runs parallel to the BTC oil pipeline, was built to transport natural gas from Shah Deniz through the South Caucasus to Turkey and eventually to world markets.[12] Perhaps to neutralize Iran's claims at Shah Deniz, Azerbaijan offered and Iran accepted a 10 percent passive share in the consortium that controls the field. To support Baku, Washington even gave a sanctions wavier to this transaction.[13]

---

8. Gulnara Rzayeva, *The Outlook for Azerbaijani Gas Supplies to Europe: Challenges and Perspectives* (Oxford: Oxford Institute for Energy Studies, June 2015), 55, http://www.oxfordenergy.org/wpcms/wp-content/uploads/2015/06/NG-97.pdf. The report provides an excellent discussion of Azerbaijan's gas supplies.

9. "Iran Is Accused of Threatening Research Vessel in Caspian Sea," *New York Times*, July 25, 2001, http://www.nytimes.com/2001/07/25/world/iran-is-accused-of-threatening-research-vessel-in-caspian-sea.html.

10. The consortium includes BP (United Kingdom), 30.1%; State Oil Company of Azerbaijan (SOCAR)(Azerbaijan), 25.0%; Chevron (USA), 8.9%; Statoil (Norway), 8.71%; Türkiye Petrolleri Anonim Ortaklığı (TPAO)(Turkey), 6.53%; Eni (Italy), 5.0%; Total (France), 5.0%; Itochu (Japan), 3.4%; Inpex (Japan), 2.5%; ConocoPhillips (USA), 2.5%; and ONGC (India), 2.36%.

11. BP, "Baku-Tbilisi-Ceyhan pipeline," 2016, http://www.bp.com/en_az/caspian/operationsprojects/pipelines/BTC.html.

12. BP, "South Caucasus pipeline," 2016, http://www.bp.com/en_az/caspian/operationsprojects/pipelines/SCP.html.

13. Kenneth Katzman, "Iran's Foreign Policy," Congressional Research Service, January 29, 2015, 20, https://www.fas.org/sgp/crs/mideast/R44017.pdf.

In addition to these resource conflicts, the political relationship between Iran and Azerbaijan has occasionally been antagonistic, more so than Iran's relations with any other state in the South Caucasus or Central Asia. This is ironic, given how much the two states and peoples have in common.[14] The northern part of the modern Republic of Azerbaijan was part of Iran until the early eighteenth century, when Iran ceded it to Russia. Today, Iran and Azerbaijan are the only countries in the world where an overwhelming majority of the population adheres to the Twelver Shi'a branch of Islam. The two countries are linked by ethnicity as well as religion: approximately 20 million Azeris live in Iran, approximately twice as many as in the Republic of Azerbaijan. Since 1501, when Twelver Shi'ism was established as the state religion by Iran's Safavid dynasty, Azeris have been the most powerful minority in Iran and have played a major role in Iranian politics. Current Iranian Supreme Leader Ayatollah Ali Khamenei is an Azeri, as was Ayatollah Kazem Shariatmadari, one of the three leaders of the 1979 revolution.

Although Iran quickly recognized the independence of the Republic of Azerbaijan in 1991, it was abundantly clear from the outset that the secular Azerbaijan would keep its distance from Iran's theocratic regime and gravitate instead toward the West and Turkey. Following independence, Baku hoped to diminish its dependence on Russia and receive Western technical assistance and capital to develop its enormous oil and gas reserves.

Apart from energy issues in the Caspian, quarrels between Tehran and Baku have revolved around three issues: Iran's stance during the Nagorno-Karabakh war, Baku's occasional call for unification with the Iranian province of Azerbaijan, and Azerbaijan's growing relations with Israel.

In the war between Armenia and Azerbaijan (1988–1994) over Nagorno-Karabakh, Islamic Iran did not side with Islamic Azerbaijan—a good illustration of how pragmatism, not Islamic solidarity, has defined Iran's policy in the region.[15] Instead, Tehran mediated between the warring sides, hoping to stabilize the region and prevent wanton violence and ethnic cleansing. In fact, President Hashemi Rafsanjani brought the leaders of Armenia and Azerbaijan to Tehran in 1992 and established a fleeting cease-fire.

This Iranian posture infuriated Baku, which accused Iran of abandoning an Islamic country at war with a Christian country and behaving vindictively to punish Azerbaijan for seeking to unify with the Azeris of Iran. Whatever the merit of these allegations, there were compelling security and political imperatives for Iran not to take sides in the conflict and instead play the role of a mediator. For one, Iran did not want a lingering war on its northern borders, which could have resulted in thousands of refugees flooding the country. With more than 2 million Afghan refugees already living in Iran, the Islamic Republic sought to extinguish the fires of another destabilizing war in its neighborhood. For another, maintaining a balance of power between Azerbaijan and Armenia served Iranian national interests.[16] Tehran was disheartened at Azerbaijan's pro-Western orientation

---

14. Touraj Atabaki, *Azerbaijan: Ethnicity and the Struggle for Power in Iran* (New York: I.B. Tauris, 2000).

15. Geoffrey Gresh makes the same argument. See Gresh, "Coddling the Caucasus: Iran's Strategic Relationship with Azerbaijan and Armenia," *CRIA Caucasian Review of International Affairs* 1, no. 1 (Winter 2006), http://www.cria-online .org/1_1.html.

16. For a good discussion of Iran's role, see Abdollah Ramezanzadeh, "Iran's Role as Mediator in the Nagorno-Karabakh Crisis," in *Contested Borders in the Caucasus*, ed. Bruno Coppieters (Brussels: VUB University Press, 1996), http://poli.vub.ac.be/publi/ContBorders/eng/ch0701.htm.

and developed friendly relations with Armenia, which it regarded as a dependable partner to contain Turkey's growing influence in the region. Despite these factors, Iran, like the rest of the international community, has not recognized the de facto Nagorno-Karabakh Republic.

Much more explosive than the Nagorno-Karabakh conflict has been the call from Baku and various Azeri nationalist groups for the unification of the Republic of Azerbaijan with Iran's Azerbaijan province, which has recently been divided into East Azerbaijan, West Azerbaijan, and Ardibill. This squabble started in the early 1990s, when Abulfaz Elchibey, Azerbaijan's second president, called for unification as part of a wider nationalist, pan-Turkic approach to state-building. After Elchibey was overthrown in a June 1993 putsch, Baku became more cautious and only occasionally flirted with the idea of unification. It has, however, supported a variety of groups that champion unification, such as the South Azerbaijan National Liberation Movement and the Coordinating Council of World Azeris.[17]

Tehran has hardly been passive in the face of these calls and has strongly condemned Baku for its irredentist proclivities. Azerbaijan has in turn accused Iran of interfering in its internal affairs by supporting the Islamic Party of Azerbaijan (founded in 1991) and its leader, Movsum Samadov. Banned by Baku, the party advocates close relations with Iran and the creation of an Islamic republic in Azerbaijan. Hossein Shariatmadari, the publisher of the hard-line *Kayhan* newspaper and an adviser to Iran's Supreme Leader, has called for a referendum to allow the people of the Republic of Azerbaijan to decide if they would wish to join Iran.[18] The agitation by both sides has in recent years been effectively managed by both Baku and Tehran, and their relations have improved. Still, the issue of unification remains a source of tension between the two countries.

Another major source of tension is Azerbaijan's growing political, economic, and security ties to Israel.[19] For Tehran, this relationship poses the greatest security threat emanating from the region. Relations between Iran and Israel have been increasingly antagonistic since the Revolution of 1979, with each side perceiving the other as a sworn enemy.[20]

So when Israel moved to gain strategic depth against Iran in Azerbaijan, as Iran had done immediately after the Revolution of 1979 against Israel in southern Lebanon, Tehran reacted apoplectically. Tehran was genuinely concerned about Israel's motives and the potential for surreptitious and destabilizing activities on its borders. There were public reports that Blackwater, a private U.S. security contractor, was training commandos around Iranian borders, and that Baku had agreed to allow

17. "Report: Azerbaijan closes offices of 2 anti-Iran groups in Baku," Fars News Agency, Iran Project, July 29, 2013, http://theiranproject.com/blog/2013/07/29/report-azerbaijan-closes-offices-of-2-anti-iran-groups-in-baku/.

18. "Bergozari Referendum Al-Haq-e Jumhoriye Azerbaijan bi Iran," Fars News Agency, February 23, 2016, http://www.farsnews.com/newstext.php?nn=13920114000197.

19. For an Israeli perspective, see Brenda Shaffer, "Azerbaijan's Cooperation with Israel Goes Beyond Iran Tensions," *Washington Institute*, April 16, 2013, http://www.washingtoninstitute.org/policy-analysis/view/azerbaijans-cooperation-with-israel-goes-beyond-iran-tensions. Also see Brenda Shaffer, *Energy Politics* (Philadelphia: University of Pennsylvania Press, 2009). She is a great advocate for Azerbaijan but has been accused of conflict of interests in her works. See Casey Michel, "This Professor Refuses to Disclose Her Work for an Autocratic Regime," *New Republic*, January 22, 2015, http://www.newrepublic.com/article/120830/brenda-shaffer-refuses-disclose-conflicts-interest-columns.

20. For the best book on the topic, see Trita Parsi, *Treacherous Alliance: The Secret Dealings of Israel, Iran, and the United States* (New Haven, CT: Yale University Press, 2007).

Jerusalem to possibly use the Silalchay Military Base, located 540 miles from the Iranian border, to launch air strikes against Iranian nuclear facilities, though these reports were widely denied.[21] The statement by President Ilham Aliyev, first reported by WikiLeaks, that Azerbaijan's relations with Israel resemble an iceberg because "nine-tenth of it is below the surface," reinforced Iran's worst suspicions.[22] The signing of a $1.6 billion military deal between Israel and Azerbaijan in 2012, which included the building of Israeli drones in Azerbaijan, added to Iran's anxieties.[23] Given that the entire defense budget of Azerbaijan in 2012 was only $3 billion, the deal demonstrated the importance of Israel to Azerbaijan's military-security establishment.[24] Today, Israel has become the leading provider of weapons to Azerbaijan and its annual trade with Azerbaijan is about $5 billion, which is more than its trade with France.[25]

As Israel was improving its ties with Baku, Iranian anti-Israeli rhetoric became more venomous and its support increased for Hezbollah and various radical Palestinian groups. Israel was disparaged for a sinister plan to undermine Iran in the South Caucasus and Central Asia, turn Azerbaijan into an intelligence-gathering headquarters, and strengthen Azerbaijan's irredentist tendency toward unification with Iran's Azerbaijan.[26]

To allay Iran's suspicions about the possible use of Azerbaijani airspace for an Israeli attack, Baku signed a nonaggression pact with Tehran in 2005 that stated that "the two countries are not allowed to provide a third country with bases to attack either of them."[27] Despite this pact, the reverberations of Baku's friendship with the Jewish state continue to impact relations with Tehran. Baku, for example, accused Iranian-backed Hezbollah of attempting to bomb the Israeli embassy in Azerbaijan in 2012,[28] and later arrested 22 people on charges of spying for Iran.[29]

21. Jeremy Scahill, *Blackwater: The Rise of the World's Most Powerful Mercenary Army* (New York: Nation Books, 2007). Also see Allen Ruff and Steve Horn, "Uranium Double-Standard: The U.S., Kazakhstan, and Iran," *Nation of Change*, April 12, 2012, http://www.nationofchange.org/uranium-double-standard-us-kazakhstan-and-iran-1334236438.

22. Mark Perry, "Israel's Secret Staging Ground," *Foreign Policy*, March 28, 2012, http://foreignpolicy.com/2012/03/28/israels-secret-staging-ground/.

23. "Iran Ta Ke Khianat-e Aliyev ra Tahamol Mi Konad?/Behpadha-yi Fowq Modern-e Israel dar Azerbaijan Chi Mi Konand?," *Raberey News*, September 13, 2014, http://rahberey.com/ShowNews/ایران-تا-کی-خیانت-علی%E2%80%8C اف-را-تحمل-می کن%E2%80%8C.

24. John C. K. Daly, "Azerbaijan's Defense Spending Hits $4.8 Billion," *Silk Road Reporters*, November 25, 2014, http://www.silkroadreporters.com/2014/11/25/azerbaijan-defense-spending-hits-4-8-billion/.

25. Maayan Jaffe-Hoffman, "Azerbaijan and Israel: A Covert but Strategic Relationship," JewishPress.com, September 17, 2015, http://www.jewishpress.com/indepth/analysis/azerbaijan-israel-a-covert-but-strategic-relationship/2015/09/17.

26. Farzad Ramazani Bunesh, "Nagahi bi Ravabat-e Jumhoriye Azerbaijan ba Israel—Goftogoo ba Doctor Afshar Soleimani Kar-Shenass va Tahleelgar-e Mosa-il-e Qafqaz," International Peace Studies Centre, June 27, 2011, http://peace-ipsc.org/fa/نگاهی-به-روابط-جمهوری-آذربایجان-با-اسر/.

27. Agence France-Presse, "Iran, Azerbaijan sign non-aggression pact: IRNA," SpaceWar.com, May 16, 2005, http://www.spacewar.com/2005/050516132011.lkyy5bdc.html.

28. Barak Ravid, "Azerbaijan: Iranian, Hezbollah Operatives Arrested for Plotting Attack Against Foreign Targets," *Haaretz*, February 21, 2012, http://www.haaretz.com/israel-news/azerbaijan-iranian-hezbollah-operatives-arrested-for-plotting-attack-against-foreign-targets-1.414008.

29. CNN Wire Staff, "Azerbaijan arrests 22 it says spied for Iran," CNN.com, March 14, 2012, http://www.cnn.com/2012/03/14/world/asia/azerbaijan-spy-arrests/.

Iran's economic relations outside of the energy sector with Azerbaijan have been limited. However, this could change after the nuclear agreement with Iran. Azerbaijani president Ilham Aliyev met with Ayatollah Khamenei in 2014 and visited Tehran again in 2015.[30]

ARMENIA

Iran's relations with Armenia have been almost free of tensions. Iran quickly recognized Armenian independence in 1991 and has developed close relations with it in the subsequent two decades. Historic ties between the two countries are deep, as all of the modern Republic of Armenia was part of Iran until the early nineteenth century, when Iran ceded it to Russia. Today, there are an estimated 100,000 Armenians living in Iran, freely worshipping in their 200 churches throughout the country.[31]

Armenia is arguably the only country in the South Caucasus or Central Asia with which Iran shares some common strategic goals. Both are apprehensive about the growing regional influence of Russia and, especially, Turkey, and both are highly suspicious of what they see as Azerbaijan's hegemonic ambitions in the region. While Armenia has relied on Iran to ease the pain of the blockade imposed on the country both by Turkey and Azerbaijan, Iran has used Armenia to undermine, albeit on a very small scale, the U.S. sanctions. For Tehran, Armenia is the preferred gateway to Europe; for Armenia, Iran is a dependable counterweight against Turkey and Azerbaijan and a bridge to reach the Persian Gulf.

Trade between the two countries was about $330 million in 2014, placing Iran among the top seven biggest trading partners with Armenia.[32] For Iran, however, this trade is negligible (Table 1.1). In 2015, the two countries agreed to establish a joint commission to explore possibilities for joint projects and increased bilateral trade.[33] With the expected removal of the international sanctions on Iran in 2016, the economic relations between Iran and Armenia are likely to expand.

GEORGIA

After gaining independence in 1991, Georgia developed good relations with Iran. Like Armenia, Georgia is a small Christian country with historical ties to Iran. In fact, Iran ceded to Russia parts of Georgia in the early nineteenth century. Until the 2003 "Rose Revolution," which overthrew President Eduard Shevardnadze, bilateral relations were friendly but not extensive. Tehran did not welcome the Rose Revolution and interpreted it as an American conspiracy to bring Georgia under its security

---

30. "Ayatollah Khamenei meets with Azerbaijani president," *Rasa News Agency*, April 10, 2014, http://www.rasanews.ir /en/NSite/FullStory/News/?Id=766.

31. See Ali Omidi, "Prospects of Economic Relations Between Iran and Armenia," *Central Asia and the Caucuses Journal* 83 (2014): 35 (in Persian).

32. Ibid.

33. "Iran, Armenia Form Commission to Boost Trade," *Azbarez*, October 20, 2014, http://asbarez.com/128025/iran -armenia-form-commission-to-boost-trade/.

umbrella.[34] Fearing that the United States was planning similar schemes to overthrow the Islamic Republic, Tehran moved cautiously toward Tbilisi. There were other reasons for this hesitancy: Tbilisi was maneuvering to become an ally of the United States and join the Northern Atlantic Treaty Organization (NATO), while establishing close ties with the European Union and Israel.

Ironically, bilateral relations progressively improved after the Russian-Georgian War of 2008. The war presented Tehran with a difficult predicament. On one hand, Iran was determined not to antagonize Russia, its main ally for neutralizing the U.S. policy of containment. On the other hand, Iran was adamant in supporting the territorial integrity of Georgia, which Russia violated by recognizing the independence of the breakaway regions of Abkhazia and South Ossetia. Iran therefore remained neutral in the war, urged Moscow and Tbilisi to peacefully resolve their conflict, and refused to recognize the independence of the two breakaway provinces.

After the war, Georgia reformulated its policy toward Iran, and Iran reciprocated. Tbilisi recognized that Iran could be a counterweight against Russia, as well as an alternative source of energy.[35] When Russia cut off its supply of natural gas to Georgia in 2006, Iran came to the rescue with cheap energy supplies. Iran, too, saw Georgia as a country that could potentially help it undermine Western sanctions and, more important, as a possible transit route for carrying Iranian gas to Europe. The Iranian ambassador to Georgia, Majid Saber, echoed this line of thinking when he stated that Iran was a reliable friend of Georgia.[36] Despite the convergence of interests, political relations have remained friendly, but there has been no large-scale economic cooperation, apart from some limited advances in the areas of tourism, transportation, and agriculture.

Georgia has consistently demonstrated a willingness to improve relations with Iran. Then Georgian president Mikheil Saakashvili, for example, supported the 2010 nuclear deal brokered by Brazil and Turkey, which Washington rejected.[37] In an unprecedented move in 2012, Georgia invited an Iranian defense attaché to join U.S.-Georgia military exercises.[38] It was a symbolic but important move: Tbilisi was sending a clear message that it sought to develop close relations with both the West and Iran, something Tehran welcomed.

In 2010, Iran and Georgia signed an agreement establishing visa-free travel. In 2011, 60,000 Iranians visited Georgia.[39] The agreement increased suspicions in the West that Georgia was complacent in

---

34. Masoumeh Shaban Faryabi, "Internal and External Factors Shaping Georgia's Colored Revolution," *Central Asia and the Caucuses Journal* 63 (Autumn 2008): 138–160, http://ca.ipisjournals.ir/article_10585_d74108e81eb2d99808f82d5d55d71b83.pdf.

35. See Kornely K. Kakachia, "Iran and Georgia: Genuine Partnership or Marriage of Convenience?," PONARS Eurasia Policy Memo No. 186, George Washington University, September 2011, http://www.gwu.edu/~ieresgwu/assets/docs/ponars/pepm_186.pdf.

36. Ibid.

37. Alexei Barrionuevo and Sebnem Arsu, "Brazil and Turkey Near Nuclear Deal with Iran," *New York Times*, May 16, 2010, www.nytimes.com/2010/05/17/world/middleeast/17iran.html.

38. Molly Corso, "Georgia Invites Iran to Joint US Military Exercises," EurasiaNet.org, March 23, 2010, www.eurasianet.org/node/65170.

39. Madona Gasanova, "Iran, Georgia, and the West," *Alexander's Gas & Oil Connections*, August 20, 2012, http://www.gasandoil.com/oilaround/2012/08/iran-georgia-and-the-west.

allowing Iran to bypass the sanctions and invest in Georgia.[40] In 2013, therefore, the agreement was changed to require some visa restrictions.[41]

Economic interaction between the two countries has nevertheless remained limited. There is, however, a Joint Economic Commission, an intergovernmental body that works to increase trade between the two countries. Iranian exports to Georgia were about $99.4 million in 2011, which was negligible for both countries. A major obstacle for expansion of economic ties has been Western sanctions on Iran and the broader U.S. containment policy. As John Bass, U.S. ambassador to Georgia, said in 2012, "Washington does not want Georgia to be the place where Iranian companies are able to avoid international sanctions."[42]

TURKMENISTAN

Turkmenistan is arguably Iran's closet partner in Central Asia. Iran was the first country to recognize Turkmenistan, a country with which it shares a long border. Despite some disagreements, such as the dispute over the legal status of the Caspian Sea, the relationship between Tehran and Ashgabat has been friendly and cooperative.[43]

In the same way it views Armenia as the gateway to Europe, Iran sees Turkmenistan as the gateway to Central Asia. Turkmenistan is Iran's number-one trading partner among the eight countries in Central Asia and the South Caucasus, and Iran is Turkmenistan's second largest trading partner, after Russia. In a meeting with Turkmen president Gurbanguly Berdimuhamedow in Tehran in 2015, Iranian president Hassan Rouhani pledged to deepen Iran's friendship with Turkmenistan and increase the volume of bilateral trade from its current $3.6 billion to $60 billion in 10 years.[44] This projection is highly ambitious, if not unrealistic, but it does show the determination of both countries to expand their economic ties. Turkmenistan, like other Central Asian countries, is likely to benefit from the removal of sanctions on Iran.

One source of friction is pipelines. Turkmenistan supports the proposed Trans-Caspian Gas Pipeline (TCGP) that would link Turkmenistan under the Caspian Sea to Azerbaijan and on to Turkey and Europe. Iran opposes TCGP because the pipeline would bypass Iran. Turkmenistan also has strongly lobbied in favor of the proposed 1,800-kilometer Turkmenistan-Afghanistan-Pakistan-India (TAPI) natural gas pipeline, which would bypass Iran and must pass through the two unstable

---

40. Benoit Faucon, Jay Solomon, and Farnaz Fassihi, "As Sanctions Bite, Iranians Invest Big in Georgia," *Wall Street Journal*, June 20, 2013, http://www.wsj.com/articles/SB10001424127887323864304578320754133982778.

41. Cristina Maza, "Between Israel and Iran: Georgia's Delicate Diplomacy," *Balkanist*, April 30, 2014, http://balkanist.net/israel-iran-georgias-delicate-diplomatic-balancing-act/.

42. Gasanova, "Iran, Georgia, and the West."

43. Ashgabat was called Eshgh'abad in Persian, which means "the city of Love." The city was part of Persia and was ceded to Russia in the nineteenth century.

44. "Iran to Boost Trade Ties with Turkmenistan: Rouhani," Tasnim News Agency, March 11, 2015, http://www.tasnimnews.com/en/news/2015/03/11/682976/iran-to-boost-trade-ties-with-turkmenistan-rouhani; and State News Agency of Turkmenistan, "Talks Between President Gurbanguly Berdimuhamedov and President Hassan Rouhani," *Turkmenistan: The Golden Age*, March 11, 2015, http://www.turkmenistan.gov.tm/_eng/?id=4564.

regions of Kandahar in Afghanistan and Quetta in Pakistan.[45] Tehran has vehemently opposed this pipeline and has instead proposed a pipeline from Central Asia through Iran to India. That pipeline, Iran insists, would be shorter and safer than the proposed TAPI pipeline.[46] With the landmark nuclear deal with Iran, Turkmenistan is getting nervous that Iran will emerge as a competitor for the South Asian markets it is targeting. Ashgabat is therefore intensifying its efforts to finalize a deal on TAPI before the sanctions are lifted.[47]

The two countries also jointly built the Dousti Dam, which in Persian means friendship, on the Hariroud River in 2005 on their borders. They have equal access to the dam, which may be used for a variety of functions, including irrigation and hydroelectric power.

Once the international sanctions on Iran are lifted in the early 2016, the existing economic ties between Iran and Turkmenistan are likely to be strengthened and expanded.

KAZAKHSTAN

Relations between Iran and Kazakhstan have generally been cordial, but not without friction.[48] There have been limited economic exchanges between the two countries. In 2013, trade between Kazakhstan and Iran was about $620 million. However, bilateral trade fell to $209 million in 2015, probably because of Western sanctions on Iran and the decline in oil and gas prices.[49] Iranian foreign direct investment (FDI) in Kazakhstan totaled $123 million in 2014, while Kazakhstan's direct investment in Iran was $10.4 million.[50] Iran's major exports to Kazakhstan are food, chemicals, construction materials, and some industrial products. Relatively rich in natural oil reserves, Kazakhstan has engaged in a few energy swap deals with Iran. However, those deals were stopped 2011, mostly because of Western sanctions. The likelihood of the resumption of these swap arrangements has substantially increased with the resolution of Iran's nuclear impasse. The two countries cooperated to revive elements of the old Silk Road, with the

---

45. For good background information about this proposed pipeline, see "Turkmenistan-Afghanistan-Pakistan-India Gas Pipeline: South Asia's Key Project," *PetroMin Pipeliner* (April–June 2011), https://elordenmundial.files.wordpress .com/2013/02/tap-pipeline.pdf.

46. For the discussion of the politics of this pipeline, see Milani, "Iran's Policy Towards Afghanistan," 235–256. There is also the Peace Gas Pipeline that Iran has started building. It originates from the Persian Gulf and goes to Pakistan and ultimately to India. The project was delayed because of U.S. sanctions. China has now agreed to build the pipeline for $2 billion. See "China to Build $2bn Iran-Pakistan Pipeline—Media," RT.com, April 9, 2015, https://www.rt.com/business /248313-china-iran-pakistan-gas-pipeline/.

47. Micha'el Tanchum, "Turkmenistan Pushes Ahead on TAPI Pipeline," *Diplomat*, September 23, 2015, http:// thediplomat.com/2015/09/turkmenistan-pushes-ahead-on-tapi-pipeline/; and Aynur Karimova, "Turkmenistan's energy sector on agenda in London," *AzerNews*, September 30, 2015, http://www.azernews.az/region/88313.html.

48. Elaheh Kooalee, Amir Ebrahimi, and Simin Shirazi Mougouee, "Iran and Kazakhstan Relations: A Geopolitical Analysis," *Iranian Review of Foreign Affairs* 4, no. 4 (Winter 2014): 89–112.

49. "Afzayesh-e 50 dar Sad-i Saderat-e Iran bi Kazakhstan / Gandom Sadr-nisheen Varedat," Golestan Chamber of Commerce Industries, Mines, and Agriculture, http://gccim.com/Pages.aspx?CatId=259.

50. John C. K. Daly, "Kazakhstan Draws Closer to Iran," *Silk Road Reporters*, September 20, 2014, http://www .silkroadreporters.com/2014/09/20/kazakhstan-draws-closer-iran/#sthash.mPOWsXqX.dpuf.

completion of the Iran-Kazakhstan-Turkmenistan railway, discussed earlier, a good example of that cooperation.

Political relations between Tehran and Astana have been subtly tense, mostly because of the suspicion that Iran was interested in hiring Kazakhstan's scientists for its nuclear program and gaining access to Kazakhstan's rich uranium mines. An unidentified member of the International Atomic Energy Agency accused Iran of seeking to import 1,350 tons of purified uranium ore from Kazakhstan.[51] This suspicion explains why Astana has been cautious in its dealings with Iran. In 2012, Kazakh president Nursultan Nazarbayev wrote an article about what Iran can learn from Kazakhstan's experience with nuclear weapons and why he favors creating "a nuclear-free zone in Central Asia." In the article, he implied that the resolution of Iran's nuclear impasse would improve relations between Iran and Kazakhstan.[52] Two years later, Kazakhstan hosted one round of negotiations with the P5+1 (the UN Security Council's permanent five members, plus Germany) on Iran's nuclear program. After the nuclear deal was struck with Iran in 2015, reports emerged that Washington favors sending Iran's uranium to Kazakhstan.[53] The relationship between Iran and Kazakhstan is likely to improve in the coming years.

TAJIKISTAN

Theoretically, Iran should have the closest relations in Central Asia with Tajikistan, a country with which it has the most historical, cultural, and linguistic ties.[54] Former Iranian president Ahmadinejad used to say "Iran and Tajikistan are one spirit in two bodies." Unlike so many of his hyperbolic assertions, there is much truth to that proposition. Tajiks, like Iranians and many Afghanis, speak the Persian language and celebrate Nowruz, the vernal equinox, marking the beginning of the new year. Today, there appears to be some popular support in Tajikistan for reviving the Persian alphabet, which Moscow replaced with Cyrillic in the 1930s.

Despite these commonalities and despite Tajik president Emomali Rahmon stating that "Iran and Tajikistan are strategic partners," the relationship between the two countries has been friendly but far from a strategic alliance. The two countries share a common interest in defeating violent Sunni extremism and have cooperated against Sunni extremist groups. Recently, for example, Tajikistan arrested a few members of Jundollah, a Sunni Baluchi terrorist organization

---

51. Ariel Farrar-Wellman and Robert Frasco, "Kazakhstan-Iran Foreign Relations," *AEI Iran Tracker*, July 19, 2010, http://www.irantracker.org/foreign-relations/kazakhstan-iran-foreign-relations. In the same article, the annual bilateral trade is reported to exceed $2 billion in 2011, which seems inaccurate.

52. Nursultan Nazarbayev, "What Iran Can Learn from Kazakhstan," *New York Times*, March 25, 2012, http://www.nytimes.com/2012/03/26/opinion/what-iran-can-learn-from-kazakhstan.html?_r=2.

53. Laurence Norman and Jay Solomon, "Iran, U.S. Seek Deal to Send Enriched Uranium to Kazakhstan," *Wall Street Journal*, December 8, 2015, http://www.wsj.com/articles/iran-seeks-arrangement-to-send-enriched-uranium-to-kazakhstan-1449612712.

54. See Davood Kiani, "Iran and Central Asia: A Cultural Perspective," *Iranian Review of Foreign Affairs* 4, no. 4 (Winter 2014): 113–138.

that has killed more members of the Iranian Islamic Revolutionary Guards Corps than any other entity.[55]

Iran has, however, faced stiff resistance to efforts at expanding its influence in Tajikistan through cultural diplomacy.[56] Any move by Iran to expand its influence has been viewed in the West with suspicion and alarm.[57] Nor have Russia, China, and Turkey welcomed Iran's influence in Tajikistan, cultural or otherwise. Iran's most ambitious economic project in the country was a 2012 pledge to build an industrial city close to Dushanbe with some 50 enterprises. It is not clear when the project will be completed. Alexander Sodiqov writes that "experts suggest that excessive red tape and corruption prevent many Iranian investment projects in the country from materializing. More fundamentally, Iranian investors do not have the same level of protection and access to key decision-makers in Tajikistan as Russian and Chinese companies."[58] Even if Persian is the official language of Tajikistan, there is only one Iranian school, compared to at least seven Turkish schools. Iran has been unable to establish a university or a Persian TV channel, even though Persian music and movies are hugely popular in Tajikistan.

Dushanbe has been cautious not to get too close to Iran, as it is determined to maintain good relations with the West, Russia, China, and Turkey, all of which view Iran with some degree of suspicion and mistrust. Moreover, Tajikistan, with its majority Sunni population and its secular government, has been circumspect in its dealings with Iran's theocratic Shi'a government, fearing the spread of revolutionary Islam in its Shi'a version through cultural and political means. Although Iran played the role of a mediator between the warring factions in Tajikistan's 1992–1997 civil war, Dushanbe accused Iran of supporting the opposition Islamic Renaissance Party, an allegation Tehran denied.

As a result of these restraining factors, economic relations between the two countries have been neither deep nor extensive. Iranian investments in Tajikistan are estimated at around $300 million. Trade between the two countries is estimated to range from $200 million to $400 million a year, which is fairly negligible among Iran's overall foreign trade. Iranian exports include construction materials, foodstuffs, medicine, and some industrial products. Iran is very much interested in getting aluminum from Tajikistan.[59] There are no direct energy-related projects between the two countries, although Iran provides an unspecified amount of crude oil to Turkmenistan for refining and then transportation to Tajikistan.[60] A few minor joint projects have been completed as well.

---

55. Katzman, "Iran's Foreign Policy," 21.

56. For an interesting article on how some Central Asian counties look at Iranian cultural diplomacy, see E. Holikov, "Understanding Iran's Television and Radio Programs Towards Central Asia," *Advanced Science Journal* 4 (2015): 25–28, http://advancedscience.org/2015/4/025-028.pdf.

57. Brenton Clark, "Persian games: Iran's strategic foothold in Tajikistan," *OpenDemocracy*, April 10, 2012, https://www.opendemocracy.net/od-russia/brenton-clark/persian-games-iran's-strategic-foothold-in-tajikistan.

58. Alexander Sodiqov, "Iran's Latest Investment Raises Questions in Tajikistan," *CACI Analyst*, March 7, 2012, http://old.cacianalyst.org/?q=node/5735.

59. "Sarmaye-Gozari 300 million-I Iran Dar Tajikistan /Taqviyat-e Hamkari-haye Nafti Dushanbe Tehran," Fars News Agency, September 12, 2015, http://www.farsnews.com/newstext.php?nn=13940620000430.

60. Ibid.

Built by the Iranian Saber International consortium and opened in March 2006, the Anzob Tunnel connects Dushanbe to Khujand, allowing Tajikistan to connect its northern and southern regions without having to cross the territory of Uzbekistan (which has halted traffic at times over political disputes).[61] Iran also completed the Sangtoudeh-II power plant, with a 220-megawatt capacity, in Tajikistan in 2015, and has connected it to that country's national power grid.[62]

KYRGYZSTAN AND UZBEKISTAN

Relations with Kyrgyzstan and Uzbekistan are arguably Iran's lowest priority in Central Asia.

Tehran continues to have friendly relations with Kyrgyzstan, despite that country's good relations with Washington. Until 2014, Kyrgyzstan, for example, allowed the United States to operate a military base at Manas International Airport for supporting the International Security Assistance Force in Afghanistan, which largely supported the U.S. effort to defeat the Taliban and al Qaeda in Afghanistan. This did not create any tension with Tehran.[63]

Kyrgyz president Almazbek Atambayev and Iranian president Hassan Rouhani have pledged greater cooperation in fighting violent extremism and terrorism, particularly against the Islamic Movement of Uzbekistan, which has committed terrorist operations inside Uzbekistan and Kyrgyzstan. Despite this pledge, it is unclear how the two countries are cooperating against terrorism in practice.

With a small population, few natural resources, and with the smallest economy of any Central Asian country (see Table 1.1), Kyrgyzstan's economic relations with Iran have been insignificant. There is a huge and strange variation in the estimated trade between Kyrgyzstan and Iran: between $7 million and $8 million annually to $600 million annually (the International Monetary Fund reported a trade volume of $283 million for 2013).[64] Iranian officials have recently suggested that Iran is prepared to invest over $10 billion in Kyrgyzstan, a goal that seems highly unrealistic. Iran mainly exports clothing, nuts, paints, and flooring to Kyrgyzstan and imports meat and grain. There have been no major joint energy or economic projects, although the two countries have signed many agreements and have pledged to expand relations, mostly to no avail. The two countries have pledged to cooperate to facilitate Kyrgyzstan's access to the Persian Gulf.[65] As a full member of the Shanghai Cooperation Organization, Kyrgyzstan will vote

---

61. "Envoy: Iran to complete Tajikistan's independence tunnel by next year," Fars News Agency, Iran Project, March 8, 2014, http://theiranproject.com/blog/2014/05/08/envoy-iran-to-complete-tajikistans-independence-tunnel-by-next -year/.

62. "Sarmaye-Gozari 300 million-I Iran Dar Tajikistan."

63. Mary Chastain, "U.S. Leaves Military Base in Kyrgyzstan as Polish Leaders Want a Major U.S. Base in Poland," Breitbart, June 4, 2014, http://www.breitbart.com/national-security/2014/06/04/us-leaves-military-base-in-kyrgyzstan -as-polish-leaders-want-a-major-us-base-in-poland/.

64. IMF figures from Direction of Trade Statistics (DOTS) database.

65. "Qadrdani-ye Atambayev Az Movafeqat-e Iran Baray-e Sakht-e Nirogah-e Barq Abi Dar Kyrgyzstan / Rouhani: Dar Khasoos-e Yek Barnameh 10 Sal-e Hamkari Do-taraf Tavafoq Kardeem," Mizan Online, September 5, 2015, http://www.mizanonline.ir/fa/news/73484/قدردانی-آتامبایف-از-موافقت-ایران-برای-ساخت-نیروگاه-برق-آبی-در-قرقیزستان-روحانی در-خصوص-یک-برنامه-١٠ساله-همکاری-دوطرفه-توافق-کردیم.

on Iran's request to become a full member, which is one reason Tehran has been trying to improve ties with Bishkek.[66]

Iran's relations with Uzbekistan are lukewarm at best. Even though it is estimated that some 12 million of Uzbekistan's 30 million people speak the Persian (i.e., Tajik) language, there have been limited cultural exchanges between the two countries. Iranian tourism to Uzbekistan, for example, is negligible, even though the cities of Samarkand and Bukhara have a unique and sentimental place in Iranian poetry and cultural history.[67]

Nor has there been much in the way of trade interactions between the two countries, despite dozens of agreements and repeated pledges by both sides to improve ties. As in many other cases, it is difficult to get accurate information on the volume of trade between Iran and Uzbekistan. The International Monetary Fund (IMF) gives a figure of $136 million for 2013. Another source, though, reports it to be $250 million annually,[68] while a third source calculates Iran's nonoil exports to Uzbekistan at $47 million and its nonoil imports from Uzbekistan at just $14 million for 2015.[69]

66. "Takeed-e Rouhani Ber-Gostaresh-e Hamkari-ye Iqtisadi va Amniyat ba Kyrgyzstan," PressTV, September 5, 2015, http://www.presstv.ir/DetailFa/2015/09/05/427808/iran-rouhani-Kyrgyzstan.

67. "Rouhani: Iran, Uzbekistan Can Cooperate in Counter-Terrorism," Tasnim News Agency, October 27, 2015, http://www.tasnimnews.com/en/news/2015/10/27/899856/rouhani-iran-uzbekistan-can-cooperate-in-counter-terrorism.

68. "Iran, Uzbekistan sign agreement on transit discount," *Tehran Times*, November 8, 2015, http://www.tehrantimes.com/Index_view.asp?code=250673.

69. Mohammad Derakhshan Mobarakeh, "Chalesh-ha va Cheshmandaz-ha-ye Ravabat-e Iran va Uzbekistan," Vista News Hub, http://vista.ir/article/250224/چالش-ها-و-چشم-اندازهای-روابط-ایران-و-ازبکستان.

03

Iran in a Reconnecting Eurasia

Geographic location might not be destiny in international politics, but its critical role is undisputable. In comparison with the post-Soviet states of Eurasia, Iran is blessed with an advantageous strategic location, which it has historically used to expand its influence. One of Iran's key priorities has consequently been revitalizing the old Silk Road, which stretched from the Mediterranean Sea across Eurasia to China. Tehran, in collaboration with the regional states, has consequently sought to build the necessary infrastructure, including roads, railways, and natural gas and oil pipelines. The more the West sought to contain Iran and exclude it from the lucrative energy projects in Central Asia and the South Caucasus, the more Iran was forced to focus on reviving connections along the old Silk Road, while engaging in small and medium-size economic and energy-related projects in its northern neighborhood. Iran's performance on these counts has, however, been mixed at best.

RAILWAYS

As part of its efforts to revive the old Silk Road, Iran has placed significant emphasis on building railroads, and has worked together with Turkmenistan on many of them.[1] Iran and Turkmenistan cooperated to build the Mashhad-Sarakhs-Tajan railway in 1996.[2] The railway was the first step to link landlocked Central Asia to the Persian Gulf through the Iranian railway system.[3] To increase trade, Iran also established the Sarakhs Free Zone, located on the border between the two counties.[4]

1. "Iran-Turkmenistan-Kazakhstan rail link inaugurated," *Railway Gazette*, December 4, 2014, http://www.railwaygazette .com/news/news/asia/single-view/view/iran-turkmenistan-kazakhstan-rail-link-inaugurated.html.

2. Sarah Chowdhry, "Iran-Turkmenistan railway launched," UPI, May 13, 1996, http://www.upi.com/Archives/1996/05 /13/Iran-Turkmenistan-railway-launched/3801831960000/.

3. See Hussein Al-Nadeem, "Iran Inaugurates Rail Link to Revive the Ancient Silk Road," *Executive Intelligence Review* 23, no. 26 (June 21, 1996): 11–13, http://www.larouchepub.com/eiw/public/1996/eirv23n26-19960621/eirv23n26 -19960621_011-iran_inaugurates_rail_link_to_re.pdf.

4. "Iran's Sarakhs Trade Zone Welcomes Foreign Investment," Fars News Agency, November 7, 2014, http://english .farsnews.com/newstext.aspx?nn=13930816000619.

Much more consequential was the completion in 2014 of the strategic Iran-Kazakhstan-Turkmenistan railway that connects landlocked Central Asia to the Persian Gulf.[5] The presidents of Iran, Kazakhstan, and Turkmenistan joined to celebrate the inauguration of the 930-kilomter railroad that connects the three countries and reduces by 600 kilometer the transportation distant from Beyneu in Western Kazakhstan to Meshad, Iran. The railroad, which initially had the capacity to transport 5 million tons per year, has the potential to carry 20 million tons per year by 2020.[6] The economic benefits of the new railroad are enormous as it is would increase trade among the three countries and would allow the landlocked Central Asian countries to reach international markets via Iran.

In 2013, Armenia awarded a $3 billion contract to a Dubai-based investment company, Rasia, to build the planned South Armenian Railway.[7] The railway would provide the shortest transportation route from the Black Sea through Iran to the Persian Gulf. When completed, this route could be a transformative project in the South Caucasus and would create new business opportunities for both Armenia and Iran. For Armenia, the railway would also neutralize the blockade by Azerbaijan and Turkey, allowing direct access to Iranian and Persian Gulf markets.[8]

PIPELINES

Even though Iran has some of the world's largest reserves of natural gas, it lacks internal connections between its principal gas fields in the south and population centers in the north. It consequently remains dependent to a significant extent on imports, especially through pipelines running from neighboring states in Central Asia. Iran also exports its own gas to neighboring Armenia, which depends on economic linkages to Iran and Russia given the closure of its borders with Azerbaijan and Turkey.

The Korpeje-Kordkuy pipeline, for example, is a 200-mile-long natural gas pipeline from Korpeje field in Turkmenistan to Kordkuy in Iran. Completed in 1997, the pipeline, which has the potential to eventually transport gas to Turkey and Europe, exports about 8 billion cubic meters of gas a year to Iran, with the potential to increase to 14 bcm. There is also a smaller Dauletabad-Sarakhs-Khangiran pipeline that was built to supply Turkmen natural gas to Iran's domestic market.

The cooperation in the energy sector has been mutually beneficial to both sides. It has allowed Turkmenistan to export its oil and gas and reduce its debilitating dependence on Russia's distribution system and, more recently, on pipelines to China as well. When built, for example, the Korpeje-Kordkuy pipeline was the "only natural gas pipeline from Turkmenistan not dependent

5. Daly, "Kazakhstan Draws Closer to Iran."

6. Joanna Lillis, "Kazakhstan, Turkmenistan, and Iran Launch Railroad to Get Trade on Track," EurasiaNet.org, December 3, 2014, http://www.eurasianet.org/node/71166.

7. "Dubai-based Investment Company, Rasia, Awarded $3 Billion Railway and High Speed Road Projects in Armenia," PR Newswire, January 24, 2013, http://www.prnewswire.com/news-releases/dubai-based-investment-company-rasia-awarded-3-billion-railway-and-high-speed-road-projects-in-armenia-188188411.html.

8. Erick Davtyan, "Iran and Armenia Expand Strategic Cooperation," *New Eastern Europe*, February 16, 2015, http://www.neweasterneurope.eu/articles-and-commentary/1492-iran-and-armenia-expand-strategic-co-operation.

upon Russia."[9] The bilateral cooperation has allowed Iran to slightly circumvent the Western sanctions, lessen its isolation, and distribute oil and gas to its northeastern provinces.

Completed in 2008, the 87-mile-long Iran-Armenia Gas Pipeline transports gas from Tabriz in Iran to Armenia.[10] Operated on the basis of a gas-for-electricity swap, the pipeline has the potential to reach beyond Armenia. (Iran has tried to find creative ways to circumvent the U.S. sanctions, such as doing barter interactions as well as swap deals in which Iran would receive gas or oil from states in the region and, in exchange, would sell an equal amount of gas or oil for them through the Persian Gulf.) Yerevan welcomed the swap deal because it diminished its dependency on Russian gas. The deal allowed Iran to export its gas and circumvent sanctions and receive badly needed electricity. Russia's Gazprom, however, bought the Armenian section of the pipeline in 2015, thus shattering Armenia's dream of energy independence as well as Iran's hope to export its gas through Armenia and Georgia and the Ukraine to Europe.[11]

In 2015, Iran and Azerbaijan also declared their willingness to carry out swap deliveries of Azerbaijani oil to the Persian Gulf, announcing that "Iran can use Azerbaijan's infrastructure, especially the Baku-Tbilisi-Ceyhan pipeline to export its oil" to Europe.[12] Azerbaijan also has invited Iran to join the Trans-Anatolian Pipeline (TANAP), which connects the Shah Deniz natural gas field in Azerbaijan through Georgia and Turkey to Europe. Iran is studying the offer.[13] The two countries have also signed a number of agreements in the past three years to jointly build roads and hydroelectric power plants.[14]

9. Geoffrey Kemp, "U.S.-Iranian Relations: Competition or Cooperation in the Caspian Sea Basin," in *Energy and Conflict in Central Asia and the Caucasus*, ed. Robert Ebel and Rajan Menon (Lanham, MD: Rowman & Littlefield, 2000), 154.

10. "Iran-Armenia gas pipeline inaugurated," *Tehran Times*, December 4, 2008, http://www.tehrantimes.com/index_View.asp?code=183993; and Vladimir Socor, "Iran-Armenia Gas Pipeline: Far More Than Meets the Eye," *Eurasia Daily Monitor* 4, no. 56 (March 21, 2007), http://www.jamestown.org/single/?no_cache=1&tx_ttnews%5Btt_news%5D=32607#.VivvJH-9KSM.

11. "Armenia to sell Iran gas pipeline to Gazprom," PressTV, June 5, 2015, http://www.presstv.com/Detail/2015/06/05/414428/Iran-gas-armenia-pipeline-ga; and Giorgi Lomsadze, "Gazprom to Take Over Iranian-Armenian Pipeline," EurasiaNet.org, June 4, 2015, http://www.eurasianet.org/node/73731.

12. "Baku Offers New Routes, Pipelines for Iran Energy Export," *Financial Tribune*, August 6, 2015, http://financialtribune.com/articles/energy/22824/baku-offers-new-routes-pipelines-iran-energy-export; and "Tehran, Baku plan extended energy cooperation: Deputy oil min.," PressTV, August 4, 2015, http://www.presstv.com/Detail/2015/08/04/423240/iran-azerbaijan-Irans-Oil-Minister-Bijan-Zanganeh-Azerbaijans-Minister-of-Economic-Development-Shahin-Mustafayev-.

13. "Iran can join TANAP pipeline to export natural gas to Europe: Azeri energy min.," PressTV, June 3, 2015, http://www.presstv.com/Detail/2015/06/03/414163/iran-natural-gas-Azerbaijan-minister-of-energy-Natig-AliyevTransAnatolian-Pipeline-TANAP.

14. "Iran, Azerbaijan sign agreement," Mehr News Agency, Iran Project, April 9, 2014, http://theiranproject.com/blog/2014/04/09/iran-azerbaijan-sign-agreement/.

Conclusion

Has the Islamic Republic of Iran achieved its major goals in Central Asia and the South Caucasus? The record is mixed, at best.

AMBITIONS AND ACHIEVEMENTS

More than a quarter of century after the collapse of the Soviet Union and the establishment of the eight new republics in the South Caucasus and Central Asia, Iran has, despite Western sanctions and the U.S. containment strategy, succeeded in developing excellent relations with Armenia, Iran's gateway to Europe, and with Turkmenistan, Iran's gateway to Central Asia. Iran also has established good relations with Georgia, Azerbaijan, Tajikistan, and Kazakhstan and has cordial relations with Kyrgyzstan and Uzbekistan.

Today Iran has a few dependable friends in the two regions, but it does not, perhaps with the exception of Armenia, have any strategic allies. Although some of the states of the South Caucasus and Central Asia initially hoped to rely on Iran to gain energy independence from Russia, and although they all share with Iran the goal of defeating violent Sunni extremism, none of them has become a strategic partner of Iran. On one hand, Washington has pressured these countries not to get too close to Tehran, and on the hand, Russia and Turkey are determined to sustain their power in the South Caucasus and Central Asia by preventing Iran from exercising real influence there.

In terms of Tehran's own strategic goals, it has succeeded in becoming a very influential player that cannot be ignored and has managed its relations with the eight states to avoid the eruption of any major conflict. Today, there is no imminent threat to Iran emanating from Central Asia or the South Caucasus, although Baku's growing military-security relations with Israel remain a major security concern for the Islamic Republic.

Iran has yet to finalize a resolution regarding the legal status of the Caspian Sea that protects its interests. If anything, it seems increasingly clear that Iran has abandoned, if not surrendered, its original position of maintaining the 1921 treaty with the Soviet Union in which the riches of the Caspian Sea would be shared equally among the five littoral states.

Iran's energy ambitions have also fallen short. It has been unable to establish itself as an energy hub for the region or to export its natural gas and oil to Europe from its southern borders, or to connect, through pipelines, the Caspian Sea to the Persian Gulf and the Gulf of Oman. Iran has established a number of oil and gas swaps, but they have been small in scale and comparatively inconsequential. As a result of Western sanctions, moreover, Iran has been totally excluded from the huge pipelines being built and proposed across the region to transport oil and gas to international markets.

Iran has done fairly well to expand and connect its railway networks, roads, and tunnels to revive the old Silk Road, connecting Iran to China and India through Central Asia and to Europe through the South Caucasus. The completion of the 930-kilometer Iran-Kazakhstan-Turkmenistan railway in 2014, which connects landlocked Central Asia to the Persian Gulf, is perhaps the most consequential of these efforts.

Iran has also cooperated and collaborated with the states of the South Caucasus and Central Asia to combat violent jihadism and terrorism. It has been active in the ECO and has made progress in upgrading its status from an observer to a full member in the Shanghai Cooperation Organization.

Finally, and perhaps most important, Iran has been able to partially undermine the sanctions regime imposed by the West. Though a variety of creative methods, such as bartering or swap deals, Iran caused some cracks on the sanctions regime, even if such cracks were not in critical areas.

THE NUCLEAR DEAL'S AND IRAN'S RELATIONS WITH THE SOUTH CAUCASUS AND CENTRAL ASIAN STATES

The landmark nuclear agreement between Iran and the six global powers (P5+1) is a potentially transformative political event that could change the landscape of the greater Middle East in the coming years.[1] Its political impact will be felt throughout Eurasia as well, although its effects might not be as dramatic there as in the greater Middle East. Even if the nuclear agreement remains exclusively an arms-control deal, as hard-liners in both Tehran and Washington seek, its impact will be moderately significant. The lifting of the sanctions regime on Iran expected in 2016 would create enticing new opportunities for Tehran throughout Eurasia. If the nuclear deal is expanded to include a political rapprochement between Iran and the United States/West, as presidents Obama and Rouhani hope, then its political impact would be huge, in Eurasia as elsewhere.

In late 2015, the International Monetary Fund released its report about the economic implications and consequences of Iran's nuclear agreement. The report concludes that "Iran's return to the global oil markets is expected to increase global supply of oil, and the removal of sanctions is likely

1. I discuss the implications of this deal in Mohsen Milani, "On Iranian Politics After the Deal: Why It Is Time for Optimism," *Foreign Affairs*, July 15, 2015, https://www.foreignaffairs.com/articles/iran/2015-07-15/iranian-politics-after-deal.

to open new trade and investment opportunities."[2] It goes on to project that nonoil trade between Iran and its neighbors, including the countries in Central Asia and the South Caucasus, will increase and Iran's "trading partners stand to gain from increased trade with Iran."

In terms of natural gas, the IMF report concludes that Azerbaijan's gas cooperation with Iran is "likely to continue [in] the future" and its trade with Iran is likely to increase. Trade with Kazakhstan, which had increased during the sanctions, is expected to increase further, with future openings in particular for new infrastructure projects. For Turkmenistan, it is expected that Iran can help Ashgabat diversify access to international gas markets. The IMF projects that trade could easily grow between the two counties, but that new infrastructure must be built first. Trade with Armenia and Uzbekistan is expected to increase as well. For Kyrgyzstan, there could be preferential trade agreements and a potential Afghanistan-China-Iran-Kyrgyzstan-Tajikistan railroad. With improvement in infrastructure, Tajikistan could benefit from increased trade with Iran as well, the IMF report suggests.

The nuclear agreement will gradually removal most of the economic and financial sanctions imposed on Iran. Leaders of the eight states of the South Caucasus and Central Asia have wisely recognized this new reality and appear anxious to expand relations with Iran based, as it must be, on mutual respect and noninterference in each other's internal affairs.[3] Iran is well aware of the new opportunities in the post–nuclear deal era. Iranian foreign minister Mohammad Javad Zarif, in an April 2015 joint press conference with his Kazakh counterpart, Yerlan Idrissov, declared that "no ceiling for the expansion of relations with regional countries whether in the Caucasus or in Central Asia" exists.[4]

But will Tehran demonstrate the perspicacity and the will to improve its regional position by reducing tensions with the United States and improving ties with the West? Will Tehran recalibrate, as it must, its regional policies, reallocating some of its resources from the Persian Gulf and the Levant regions to Central Asia and the South Caucasus? Only if it can, only then will Iran have a good chance to emerge as a major regional power in Central Asia and the South Caucasus, a region where its civilizational legacy and historical footprints are palpably and profoundly visible.

---

2. International Monetary Fund (IMF), *Regional Economic Outlook: Middle East and Central Asia* (Washington, DC: IMF, October 2015), 81, http://www.elibrary.imf.org/doc/IMF086/22764-9781513528526/22764-9781513528526/Other_formats/Source_PDF/22764-9781513513386.pdf?redirect=true.

3. Aynur Karimova, "Moody's expects Iran nuke deal to offer new trade opportunities for Azerbaijan," *AzerNews*, September 30, 2015, http://www.azernews.az/oil_and_gas/88276.html.

4. Catherine Putz, "Why Is Central Asia Excited About the Iran Deal?," *Diplomat*, April 15, 2015, http://thediplomat.com/2015/04/why-is-central-asia-excited-about-the-iran-deal/.

About the Author

Mohsen Milani is executive director of the Center for Strategic and Diplomatic Studies and professor of politics at the University of South Florida. He has authored more than 70 publications on Iran's revolution and its foreign policy. Since 2000, he has been invited to more than 200 conferences and workshops in 27 countries. His scholarly works have been translated into French, Japanese, Chinese, Arabic, and Persian.

www.ingramcontent.com/pod-product-compliance
Lightning Source LLC
Chambersburg PA
CBHW081438270326
41932CB00019B/3251